I0814079

FEATHERED FARM ANIMALS

QUAIL

by Elizabeth Andrews

Cody Koala
An Imprint of Pop!
popbooksonline.com

Hello! My name is Cody Koala

This book is filled with videos, puzzles, games, and more! Scan the QR codes* while you read, or visit the website below to make this book pop.

popbooksonline.com/quail

*Scanning QR codes requires a web-enabled smart device with a QR code reader app and a camera.

abdobooks.com

Published by Pop!, a division of ABDO, PO Box 398166, Minneapolis, Minnesota 55439.

Printed in the United States of America, North Mankato, Minnesota.

082025
012026

Cover Photo: Shutterstock Images
Interior Photos: Adobe Stock; Alamy Stock Photo; Getty Images; Shutterstock Images
Editors: Tyler Gieseke and Grace Hansen
Series Designer: Julia Line

Library of Congress Control Number: 2025940518

Publisher's Cataloging-in-Publication Data

Names: Andrews, Elizabeth, author.
Title: Quail / by Elizabeth Andrews
Description: Minneapolis, Minnesota : Pop!, 2026 | Series: Feathered farm animals | Includes online resources and index
Identifiers: ISBN 9781098248574 (lib. bdg.) | ISBN 9781098249090 (ebook)
Subjects: LCSH: Common quail--Juvenile literature. | Poultry--Juvenile literature. | Fowls--Juvenile literature. | Farm animals--Juvenile literature. | Animal husbandry--Juvenile literature.
Classification: DDC 636.63--dc23

Table of Contents

Chapter 1

Meet the Quail!

Quail are birds. They live in the wild and on farms in groups called flocks. Male quail are called cocks. Females are called hens. They make sounds like songbirds.

Watch a video here!

Quail are raised for their meat and eggs. Both are healthier for people than other **poultry**. There are many quail **breeds**. The most common type on farms is the coturnix quail.

Another popular quail breed is the California quail. They have head **plumes**.

Quail are the smallest farm bird. Coturnix quail usually weigh between 3.5 and

5.6 ounces (99–159 g). They are around 6.7 inches (17 cm) long. All quail breeds are little.

Quail are round and covered in feathers. Cocks and hens look similar. However, hens have speckles on their chest feathers. Cocks do not. Both have stripes on their face.

beak
wing
tail
claw

Chapter 2

Life on the Farm

Farmers keep quail in pens covered with netting so they don't fly away. These pens also keep quail safe from **predators**. They are kept in **hutches** at night.

Learn more here!

Quail live on the ground. They like to hide in **vegetation**. They don't need much space to move because they like being close together. Hens build their nests on the ground too.

Hens start laying eggs at between six and eight weeks old. This is much earlier than other **poultry**. Their eggs are

white or speckled. Hens lay an egg every day.

Some farmers give hens nesting boxes. This protects the eggs from predators.

Chapter 3

What Do They Eat?

Farmers give quail special **feed**. It is a mix of grains and other **vitamins** quail need. They also eat seeds, plants, and insects. Quail need fresh water daily.

Explore links here!

Chapter 4

Tiny Chicks

Quail babies are called chicks. They are tiny and covered with soft feathers called down. Quail chicks must live in safe, warm containers for four weeks. Then they are ready to live outside.

Chicks break out of their eggs after just 17 days.

Making Connections

Text-to-Self

What is one new thing you learned about quail in this book?

Text-to-Text

Have you read about any other farm animals? If so, how were those animals similar to or different from quail?

Text-to-World

With the help of an adult, look up a few different quail breeds. How are their appearances similar to and different from the coturnix quail's?

Glossary

breed – a specific type of an animal that is raised by humans.

feed – food designed for a specific kind of animal.

hutch – a cage for small animals, usually made of wood or wire.

plume – a large and showy feather of a bird.

poultry – farm birds raised for their meat and eggs.

predator – an animal that lives by hunting and eating other animals.

vegetation – plants or plant life.

vitamin – one of a number of natural or human-made substances needed to keep a body healthy.

Index

Online Resources

popbooksonline.com

Thanks for reading this Cody Koala book!

This book is filled with videos, puzzles, games, and more! Scan the QR codes* while you read, or visit the website below to make this book pop.

popbooksonline.com/quail

*Scanning QR codes requires a web-enabled smart device with a QR code reader app and a camera.